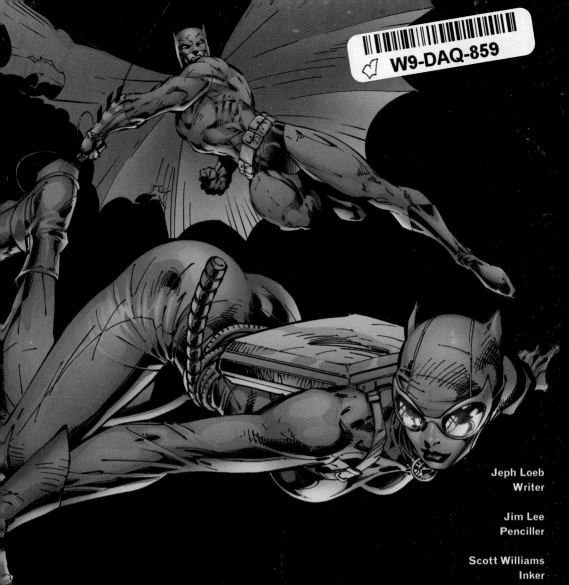

Jeph Loeb
Writer

Jim Lee
Penciller

Scott Williams
Inker

Richard Starkings
Letterer

Alex Sinclair
Colorist

Jim Lee & Scott Williams
Original Series Covers

Batman created by Bob Kane

BATMAN
VOLUME ONE
HUSH

Dan DiDio
VP-Executive Editor

Bob Schreck
Editor-Original Series

Robert Greenberger
Senior Editor-Collected Edition

Robbin Brosterman
Senior Art Director

Paul Levitz
President & Publisher

Georg Brewer
VP-Design & Retail Product Development

Richard Bruning
Senior VP-Creative Director

Patrick Caldon
Senior VP-Finance & Operations

Chris Caramalis
VP-Finance

Terri Cunningham
VP-Managing Editor

Alison Gill
VP-Manufacturing

Rich Johnson
VP-Book Trade Sales

Hank Kanalz
VP-General Manager, WildStorm

Lillian Laserson
Senior VP & General Counsel

Jim Lee
Editorial Director, WildStorm

David McKillips
VP-Advertising & Custom Publishing

John Nee
VP-Business Development

Gregory Noveck
Senior VP-Creative Affairs

Cheryl Rubin
Senior VP-Brand Management

Bob Wayne
VP-Sales & Marketing

BATMAN: HUSH VOLUME ONE

Published by DC Comics.
Cover, introduction, and compilation copyright
© 2003 DC Comics.

Originally published in single magazine form
as BATMAN 608-612. Copyright © 2002, 2003
DC Comics. All Rights Reserved.

DC Comics
1700 Broadway
New York, NY 10019

A Warner Bros. Entertainment Company
Printed in Canada.
Third Printing.

ISBN: 1 4012 0060 5

Cover illustration by Jim Lee
and Scott Williams.
Cover color by Alex Sinclair.

When I was a little boy my family would get together in my father's den every Wednesday and Thursday night at 7:30 pm to watch a new television show called *Batman*. Twice a week, Adam West and Burt Ward would BIFF! BAM! and POW! with some of Hollywood's most notables playing The Joker, The Riddler, etc. While I'd like to lay claim to remembering best Julie Newmar's sleek cat outfit as my strongest memory, it only ranks a close second. My most vivid memory was actually of my father's backside blocking the television. You see, *Batman* had a very distinct message at the bottom of the screen below the logo: IN COLOR. My father had purchased a brand-new RCA color television and spent most of the show getting up and adjusting the reds and greens (it was a very colorful show) in order to get it, as he would say, "Just right." It didn't matter that the rest of us couldn't actually tell the difference each time he got up and twisted some knob; for my Dad there was a world of difference.

What does all this have to do with HUSH? Glad you asked. On a bright and sunny California afternoon, in the parking lot of the Warner Bros. studio, I met with Mark Chiarello (DC's Editorial Art Director), who had traveled out from the not so bright or sunny New York City to see if I would be interested in writing BATMAN on a monthly basis. Mark had the good (mis)fortune of being my editor on BATMAN: DARK VICTORY, the follow-up to my other Batman opus BATMAN: THE LONG HALLOWEEN, and despite having lived through that experience still wanted to gauge my interest.

JUST RIGHT

INTRODUCTION BY JEPH LOEB

Before I answered, I asked (as I always do) the most important question any comic-book writer can ask before he takes an assignment. I don't care if you grew up reading every issue of *The Adventures of Pow Wow Jones* and this is your only chance to prove to the world that you and Pow Wow were made for each other, you have to ask:

"Who's going to draw it?"

Because, my friends, no matter how good a comic-book story is, it is still a visual medium. We don't write short stories, or novels, or poetry for that matter. We write stories that someone has to draw. And if you find yourself stuck with the unlucky reality of having someone draw your story that doesn't suit what you've got in your head, it's a little like trying to listen to a song you wrote for a piano played on a tuba. It's your song all right, it just doesn't sound ... well... "Just right."

I had a pretty good ace in the hole when I asked. I had only worked on Batman with Tim Sale, who is something of a master illustrator and has made me look better than I am on more than a few occasions. Mark knew Tim was busy. Who could Chiarello possibly come up with who was going to match my ace?

"Jim Lee."

The guy who, at a very young age, sold
more copies of a single comic book
than anyone else in history.
(A record he still holds
today — at about 8 million).

I gulped. If I had the Ace of Hearts, Mark threw down the Ace of Diamonds. Now, we can sit here until tomorrow morning and argue who was better — Michelangelo or da Vinci, but let's save the time and accept that they are both great artists. Different but, no question about it, brilliant. That's how I feel about Tim and Jim.

So, I did what any writer would do without asking how much the job paid. I said "Yes."

Now I had a bigger problem. What story was I going to tell? The greatest challenge a comic-book writer faces is making sure that the story suits the artist's strengths. (Don't forget about that tuba!). Tim and I had only told stories that took place in the mythical "Year One." This is where Batman is starting out and has no Robin or Nightwing or Oracle as part of his cadre. He makes mistakes because he's learning his detective craft, and he has an uneasy alliance with the Gotham City police force.

Jim and I were going to be working in the "Present Day" continuity of Batman. The Dark Knight's at the top of his game now, having inspired a Robin or three, Nightwing, two Batgirls, and an Oracle. Kind of like the dozens of artists who followed Jim's spectacular rocket to comic-book stardom. Gotham City is now his to protect, and he does a damn fine job of it. Kind of like the comic-book industry as a whole, and the contribution Jim has made to it as both a creator and a publisher. The trick is, when you're that good, you need a bigger challenge. Kind of like... Jim.

Where Tim works well in the shadows and ink, Jim demands that you see it all. The magic is in the details. What glorious details! Backgrounds and Batmobiles and babes! Catwoman! Poison Ivy! And... a certain Man of Steel!

I'll let you in on a little secret. No, it's not who or what is the mysterious person in the bandages who seems to have something to do with Batman's plight. This is better. Jim doesn't do his wizardry alone. Nope. He has help.

Scott Williams has inked Jim for longer than either of them likes to admit. If Jim ever needed another arm, it's Scott. Jim's pencils are good, mind you, but Scott has a way of making them glimmer. Scott is more than an inker — he's a partner and advisor. When I've asked if something looks "Just right," we've often deferred to Scott.

He just knows, um... righter.

That only gets us to the black and white of it all. Jim's handpicked colorist is Alex Sinclair. The result is the spectacular vibrancy of color you'll see throughout these chapters. If comics have made a single gigantic leap in the last sixty-odd years, it's in the area of color. Look inside and see what Alex has created!

In fairness to Jim, I can't do anything with my story without help as well. My advisor and "partner in words" is Richard Starkings, who, along with Wes Abbott, has lettered these chapters with such style that even the offbeat notes sound like sweet harmony. As you read the story, take a moment to look at the words themselves. That's Richard's gift.

None of this is possible without the amazing Bat-editorial staff, led by Morgan Dontanville and the Keeper of The Cave, Bob Schreck.

Here's the best part of all. What you hold in your hand is only part of the story. It's the first arc. We've got a grand adventure planned following these chapters and look forward to seeing you there.

Hopefully, when you've read this collection you'll sit back and relax and say to yourself, "Yep, they got it just right."

— Jeph Loeb
New Year's Day, 2003
Los Angeles, California

Suddenly orphaned and alone, a chilling event took place.

There would be no grieving for this child. No time would be lost wishing he could change these events.

There would only be *the promise.*

That very night, on the street stained with his mother and father's blood, he would make a vow to rid the city of the evil that had taken their lives.

It was, at best, a fool's errand, or so I told myself.

Using his family's wealth, Master Bruce sought out the world's greatest minds in criminology, martial arts, and the craft of detecting.

He knew that criminals are, by nature, a cowardly and superstitious lot.

In turn, he donned a cape and cowl and became a creature of the night, preying on those who broke the law.

They now call him *The Batman.*

But, I will always see him as that little boy, lost, struggling to find a way to make up for not being able to save his parents lives.

And I...? I can only offer him something I fear he sorely lacks.

Love.

6

Nails Nathan. Former C.I.A. OP. Right-handed. The poison in the tips will paralyze his hand, arm, then go to work on his head.

Tommy Harper. Gun runner for the I.R.A. Has a metal plate in his skull making him susceptible to vertigo when hit in the correct spot with *anything* magnetic.

Carlos Valdez. Chilean Mercenary. Likes to fight in close since his size makes him slow.

WHUMPPH

MARY FOR HIRE

SP

Spider Hancock. Gotham City muscle.
Broke two of his ribs three nights ago.
They won't heal any time soon.

The vanishing act involved the Gotham City sewer system.

Within six hours, a demand for ten million dollars was made. The Lamont family, the Mayor, The G.C.P.D. and even the F.B.I. all wanted to pay the ransom to get the boy back.

Everyone but *me.*

YOUR BONES WILL SNAP. YOUR BLOOD WILL FILL MY BELLY.

More than just his M.O. has changed. His body -- maybe his mind -- has mutated. As if...he were more savage than human.

That doesn't mean I'm going to let him beat the pulp out of me.

RARRR

KRACSH

What Croc has in strength and speed, he lacks in other areas.

And a vulnerability to hypersonics.

FAP

18

YEAH!

EDWARD. BE QUIET.

I never was a Boy Scout.

WHUP WHUP WHU

F.B.I. STAY WHERE YOU ARE!

NOT HOW *WE* WOULD'VE HANDLED IT --

THIS IS *MY* CITY.

EASY, SON, WE'RE GOING TO TAKE YOU HOME NOW.

...BUT...I WANT TO STAY WITH BATMAN...

-- LET ME FINISH. BUT YOU GOT RESULTS. THE BOY IS SAFE AND THE MONEY --

-- WHERE THE HELL IS THE MONEY?

I have known Catwoman... *Selina Kyle* for years.

It seems like each step we take toward each other...

...we only get further apart.

I...can smell... the gun oil... but I can't make my arms work...

HUMAN OR NOT. HE DIES NOW.

NO, H, I ONLY MEANT IN CASE YOU NEEDED BACKUP --

VROOOM

KRASH

SHUT UP, O. I *KNOW* WHAT YOU MEANT.

WHO THE --?!

GUNGH WHAK

I'M HERE.

She's better than she knows...

I'LL TAKE THAT BACK NOW.

FAP

...but wastes too much energy proving it.

NOW. BRING IT ON.

DAP

FOK

SWAG

GAH

O. WE'RE CLEAR. BUT I'M NOT SURE IF HE CAN MOVE.

So much like I was when I started out...

RUMMMBLE

!

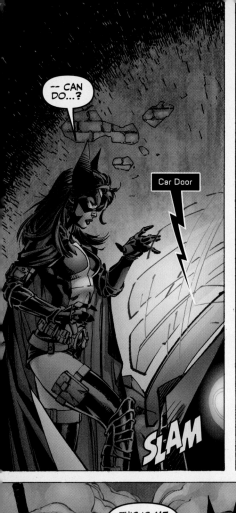

-- CAN DO...?

Car Door

SLAM

VROOOM

SKREEEEEEECH

H...

...I'M SURE WHEN HE CAN... HE'LL WANT TO THANK YOU HIMSELF.

THIS IS *ME* HOLDING MY BREATH.

"WITHOUT FRIENDS NO ONE WOULD CHOOSE TO LIVE.

"THOUGH HE HAD ALL OTHER GOODS."

CAN WE GET SOME LIGHT IN HERE?

PLANTS LIKE THE LIGHT.

IS THAT MY HALF?

YES.

AND CATWOMAN...?

NOT A PROBLEM.

BATMAN, HOWEVER, WILL --

-- HELLO...?

41

"WE MAKE WAR...

I barely survived the fall.

Had it not been for Tommy.

Had it not been for Alfred.

Had it not been for Huntress.

Had it not been for Oracle.

Had it not been... that someone cut the batrope...

"...THAT WE MAY LIVE IN PEACE."

THAT MONEY WAS MINE!

Which is why I got there first.

I rescued the boy. But *someone else* at the scene snatched the money from Croc...

BATMAN!

CROC! STEP AWAY FROM THE GLASS!

There was *no* doubt in my mind that Croc would have killed the boy even though he had the money. *That* was more his style.

THAT'S ALL RIGHT. I'M NOT HERE TO BE LIKED.

I DON'T NEED TO REMIND YOU THAT THE *FATHER* OF THE *BOY* THAT... *BEAST*...KIDNAPPED IS A *PERSONAL* FRIEND OF THE PRESIDENT.

Amanda Waller heads up President Luthor's Office of Meta-Human Affairs.

I have history with Waller. None of it pleasant.

That's all right. I'm not here to be liked either.

Dealing with anything remotely connected to Luthor makes my skin crawl. But, Croc was about to be transferred out of my city...

YOU MEAN HE'S A *MAJOR CONTRIBUTOR* TO *LUTHOR'S* CAMPAIGN PARTY.

YOU'VE GOT UNTIL *MIDNIGHT.*

THEN, CROC IS *OURS.*

KRAKA THOOM

MASTER BRUCE...?

GO AHEAD, ALFRED.

A CAR JUST PULLED UP TO THE HOUSE. ARE WE EXPECTING COMPANY?

NO.

PHILADELPHIA LICENSE PLATE. HMX 19... I CAN'T MAKE OUT THE LAST NUMBER IN THIS STORM.

I have until midnight...

Wayne Manor. What was once my father's house is now mine.

Along with all the memories that it holds.

ORACLE?

I'M HERE. EVEN OFF A PARTIAL PLATE, PHILADELPHIA D.M.V. SHOWS THE OWNER TO BE *DR. THOMAS ELLIOT.*

THAT'S... UNEXPECTED.

YOU SURE I CAN'T ENTICE YOU TO COME HOME, SIR? AFTER ALL, DR. ELLIOT *ONLY* SAVED YOUR LIFE.

I WOULD IF I COULD, ALFRED.

I BELIEVE THAT'S *"I COULD IF I WOULD,"* IN YOUR CASE, SIR.

JUST MAKE THE USUAL EXCUSE, PLEASE.

CONSIDER IT DONE, SIR.

GOOD EVEN-- TOMMY...?

HELLO, ALF.

I...I APOLOGIZE, SIR, FOR THE INFORMALITY. YOU ARE *"DOCTOR THOMAS ELLIOT"* THESE DAYS, AREN'T YOU?

BING BONG

I WILL TELL HIM...

...TOMMY...

Tommy Elliot. On a night just like this...

MASTER ELLIOT, WHAT BRINGS YOU OUT HERE AT THIS HOUR...?

ALF...

...CAN I TALK TO BRUCE?

WHAT'RE YOU DOING OUT THERE IN THE RAIN, YOU KNUCKLEHEAD?!

THERE'S... THERE'S BEEN AN ACCIDENT.

MY... MOM AND DAD... THEIR CAR...

62

Gotham City Hospital. My father was Head of Trauma Surgery back then.

Hospitals are awful places at night.

Especially for children...

MY DAD IS IN THERE, TOMMY. NOTHING BAD IS GOING TO HAPPEN.

I *TRIED* TO WARN MISTER ELLIOT.

NIGHT LIKE THIS, THE ROADS GET SLIPPERY.

I SHOULD HAVE BEEN DRIVING THEM -- BUT HE *INSISTED* ON GOING OUT ALONE WITH THE MISSUS.

YOU MUSTN'T BLAME YOURSELF, *CLARENCE. ACCIDENTS* WILL HAPPEN.

AND GIVEN THE SITUATION, THEY COULD NOT BE IN BETTER HANDS.

YOU SWEAR...?

STICK A NEEDLE IN MY EYE.

THANKS, BRUCE...

63

TOMMY.

COME HERE, SON.

YOUR MOM IS GOING TO BE JUST FINE.

SEE? I TOLDYA.

AND MY DAD...?

I...I'M SORRY. I DID EVERYTHING IN MY POWER --

NO! HE'S NOT GONE! I'M GOING IN THERE TO SEE HIM!

TOMMY, MY DAD SAID HE DID EVERYTHING --

LIAR! YOU PROMISED! YOU SWORE!

WAP

OW!

WHAT'DJA DO *THAT* FOR?

BRUCE.

BE QUIET.

WHY'D YOU HAVE TO TELL ME IT WAS GOING TO BE OKAY, BRUCE? WHY?

BERKSCH

RSKEEE

DUSSHK

HSSSSSSSSS

BATMAN!

I'M NOT GETTING -- CAN YOU HEAR ME?

THRAOOCH

ANSWER ME, DAMMIT!

ORACLE.

ARE YOU ALL RIGHT? WHAT THE HELL IS GOING ON OUT THERE?

ORACLE. WHATEVER YOU DO -- DO NOT LOSE THE HOMING SIGNAL ON CROC.

YOU DIDN'T ANSWER MY QUESTIONS --

JUST DON'T LOSE THAT SIGNAL!

...

WHUP WHUP WHUP WHUP WHUP

KILLER CROC! THIS IS THE F.B.I.!

STAY WHERE YOU ARE AND PUT YOUR HANDS IN THE AIR!

IDIOTS...

LIAR! I KNEW I COULDN'T TRUST YOU!

I'LL KILL YOU FOR THIS!

CROC! WE CAN STILL --

DAMMIT.

BAM

BUDDA BUDDA BUDDA

I'LL KILL ALL OF YOU!

looking for any clues to further my investigation.

Wherever they've stashed Croc, I can't find him...

...for now.

I keep thinking about the look in his eye just before they took him. How the monster had overcome him...

BATMAN...?

I'VE FOUND POISON IVY.

TELL ME SHE'S RELOCATED.

METROPOLIS? I WANT IN ON THIS.

LISTEN...I... YOU SAVED MY LIFE.

THROUGH THE YEARS, YOU'VE DONE THAT MORE THAN ONCE.

I DON'T THINK I'VE EVER PROPERLY THANKED YOU.

DON'T.

WE'VE DONE THIS DANCE FOR A LONG TIME. TOO LONG.

AREN'T YOU AT ALL CURIOUS?

Metropolis.

It is very different from *Gotham City* and for that alone...

...I try to avoid coming here.

There are not many reasons for *Batman* to be in this city.

But, no one will raise an eyebrow when Bruce Wayne comes to town.

Trying to stay focused.

Not to think about...

...Selina...

The last time I remember actually *wanting* to be here was years ago.

I have business interests here that I can *pretend* to look after...

I'll stop by *The Daily Planet.* It's always good to see *Lois.*

BRUCE! BRUCE WAYNE!

BRUCE! IT *IS* YOU. I'VE BEEN YELLING LIKE A FOOL HALFWAY ACROSS THE AIRPORT --

-- I'M SORRY, TOMMY -- MY MIND MUST'VE BEEN -- I WAS *JUST* THINKING ABOUT YOU.

UH-HUH. MORE LIKE YOU WERE THINKING ABOUT SKIRTS, IF HALF OF WHAT YOUR REPUTATION IS, IS TRUE.

WELL...

I kissed her...

Tommy...*Doctor Thomas Elliot.* The surgeon who saved my life and my childhood friend.

My *father* had a medical convention to attend. My *mother* thought we'd spend some time together.

My father brought *Alfred.* I brought *Tommy.*

YOU BOYS STAY *RIGHT HERE* WHILE ALFRED AND I GO REGISTER. *RIGHT* HERE, DO YOU UNDERSTAND?

YES, SIR.

YOU GOT IT, DOC.

Tommy spoke to my father in a way that no one else dared. But, that was Tommy...

DO YOU REMEMBER THE TIME WHEN *MY FATHER* BROUGHT US HERE?

SAY, YOU REALLY *WERE* THINKING ABOUT ME, AFTER ALL.

BE A SPORT AND LET'S RIDE IN TOGETHER.

UNLESS... YOU'RE MEETING SOMEONE?

Selina...

EASY, BOY. YOU PLAY YOUR CARDS RIGHT AND...

...THERE WILL BE PLENTY MORE WHERE THAT CAME FROM.

SO...I'LL SEE YOU IN *METROPOLIS*.

DID YOU EVER TELL ANYONE?

WHAT WE SAW? NOT A SOUL. STICK A NEEDLE, BRUCE.

UH... BRUCE.

LOOK. UP IN THE SKY --

WHERE --?

I made a promise on the grave of my parents to rid this city of the evil that took their lives. By day, I am Bruce Wayne, billionaire philanthropist. At night, criminals, a cowardly and superstitious lot, call me...

BATMAN

CREATED BY BOB KANE

It was one of the most extraordinary things I had ever seen in my life.

THERE! IT'S GREEN LANTERN!

HUSH

Chapter Four **THE CITY**

WHERE'D THEY GO?

DOWN THE BLOCK, C'MON --!

NO. WE SHOULD HEAD BACK.

THAT BAD GUY IS *THE ICICLE.* HE'LL *NEVER* WIN.

HOW DO YOU KNOW *THAT?*

IT'S LIKE I'M ALWAYS TELLING YOU, BRUCE. YOU GOTTA BE ABLE TO *THINK* LIKE YOUR OPPONENT.

ALFRED, BRING MY MEDICAL BAG UP TO THE --

-- WHERE ARE THE *BOYS?*

I BELIEVE THAT'S THEM COMING THIS WAY NOW, SIR.

WHAT DID I TELL YOU?

TO WAIT BY THE CAR. BUT, WE WERE JUST --

-- WE'RE NOT IN GOTHAM CITY, BRUCE.

I'M NOT ONLY RESPONSIBLE FOR *YOU,* BUT FOR YOUR *FRIEND* AS WELL.

AND SINCE *NEITHER* ONE OF YOU CAN BE TRUSTED, YOU'LL SPEND THE REST OF THE WEEKEND IN YOUR HOTEL ROOM.

We never left the room the entire time we were in Metropolis.

We stayed perched by the window, hoping to get a glimpse of another hero, but none came.

Soon after that, my parents were killed and I hardly saw Tommy again...

THINGS CHANGE.

IF WE'RE TALKING ABOUT *METROPOLIS,* IT ACTUALLY HAPPENED HERE OVERNIGHT.

CITIES ARE *MEANT* TO RISE AND FALL, BRUCE. I WAS REFERRING TO *PEOPLE.*

ANYONE IN PARTICULAR?

I'M SURE THAT ALF -- *ALFRED* TOLD YOU I CAME BY THE HOUSE.

AND I WAS SORRY TO HAVE MISSED YOU. *MONEY NEVER SLEEPS,* TOMMY --

"MONEY" ISN'T *MY* PATIENT.

YOU HAVE A FRACTURED SKULL, BRUCE. I TOOK A *BONE CHIP* OUT OF YOUR BRAIN.

I'M *GRATEFUL* --

-- I'M NOT INTERESTED IN YOUR GRATITUDE. MY *ONLY* INTEREST IS IN YOUR *HEALTH.*

I TAKE GOOD CARE OF MYSELF.

I DON'T DOUBT THAT. BUT, I'M NOT SURE YOU'VE GIVEN YOURSELF ADEQUATE TIME TO HEAL.

YOU'RE NOT *SUPERMAN,* YOU KNOW.

Catwoman...

DON'T GO.

JUST BECAUSE I LET YOU KISS ME --

--DOESN'T MEAN YOU GET TO TREAT ME LIKE YOUR *TOY* WONDER.

TAKE THIS.

IT'S NOT YOUR HIGH SCHOOL RING OR ANYTHING, IS IT?

METROPOLIS IS A BIG CITY. IF YOU FIND *POISON IVY* FIRST, ACTIVATE THAT BY PRESSING IT.

SO, I CALL, YOU COME?

YOU CAN'T TRAIN A *CAT* TO DO THAT.

OH, AND...

...IF *I* FIND IVY FIRST...?

YOU'RE GOING TO HAVE TO WAIT YOUR TURN.

I had thought about alerting Clark before we arrived.

This is *his* city.

But ... having **Selina** with me...

The reporter in him ... combined with his unflagging sense of right and wrong...

...I'm not sure he'd understand...

...and I'm sure I don't want to explain it...

88

I INTERRUPTED SOMETHING, DIDN'T I?

NOT MANY WOMEN CAN WEAR *CHANEL NO. 5* AND MAKE IT WORK.

SORRY. THAT WAS... CATTY.

I... THAT IS, *YOU* SAID --

-- THAT I WANTED TO GET TO HER FIRST. I STILL DO. BUT I WANTED YOU TO KNOW *WHY*.

I KNOW WHERE IVY IS.

SO DO I.

IVY TOOK CONTROL OF MY MIND. SHE MADE ME DO THINGS I MAY HAVE BEEN *PRONE* TO, BUT THAT'S *MY* DECISION.

NO ONE GETS TO VIOLATE ME LIKE THAT.

UNDERSTOOD?

WELL.

NOW THAT WE'RE CLEAR ON THAT.

I'LL MEET YOU THERE.

I kissed her...

In Gotham City, *Killer Croc* led me to a penthouse where he believed *Poison Ivy* would be.

The plants I found there were *Aztec gilia.* They are, at best, difficult to grow in an indoor environment.

Ivy could no more abandon them than a mother could her child, taking them with her to *Metropolis.*

I'VE COME BACK TO YOU.

HAVE YOU?

IT'S LIKE YOU SAID --

-- NO ONE CAN RESIST YOU.

YESSS...

93

...BUT I CAN *ALWAYS* TELL WHEN SOMEONE IS PRETENDING.

SRAK

THAT

WHAM

WAS

BAM

DTUSH

THE LAST TIME

THE PLANTS DON'T LIKE IT WHEN YOU TOUCH THEIR MOTHER --

-- WITCH!

VZIP

...AIR...!

IVY.

YOU ARE COMING BACK TO GOTHAM CITY.

WHAT'D YOU DO? WALK?

SO...THE KITTEN BROUGHT A CHAMPION.

GOOD.

I'VE BROUGHT MINE, TOO.

...etropolis.

W-WHAT HIT US?

HE DID.

I hate this city.

We came hunting for *Poison Ivy* for crimes she committed in *Gotham City*.

She has taken control of *Superman*.

LOVER.

KILL THEM.

TELL ME YOU HAVE A PLAN.

If I know him -- and I do --

--I know what his next move will be.

KRACK

WHERE ARE WE GOING--?!

OOM

Not yet, anyway.

THEY'RE GETTING AWAY..?

NO!

Selina is panicking. Cats and water.

She's going to have to trust me.

Nightvision Engaged.

I'm going to have to trust *her*.

WHRRR

WHRRR

NAVIGATING DISTANCE: 0.03 MILES

Given the situation it's at *best* a distraction...

...and at the worst, could get us killed.

WHOOSH

Seconds.

Poison Ivy **used** Catwoman in those Gotham City crimes.

She felt **violated** being controlled by Ivy.

It's made the hunt **personal** for Selina.

THOUGHTLESS.

WORTHLESS.

STUPID.

MAN.

I... CAN'T... KILL...

BUT, YOU ALREADY **HAVE.**

MY PLANTS ARE MY CHILDREN.

I...

ARE YOU STARTING TO **RESIST?**

FOOLISH.

NO MAN CAN RESIST ME. EVEN **SUPERMAN.**

NOW, COME CLOSER--

-- SO, I CAN **REMIND** YOU WHAT WILL MAKE **ME** HAPPY...

YOU KNOW YOUR PART?

YOUR STANDARD SNATCH AND GRAB.

ANY ONE OF THE THREE OF THEM.

IT'LL BE THE GAL. IF WE WANT TO GET A REACTION FROM HIM, IT HAS TO BE THE GAL.

000115
000115
000115
000115

YOU'VE STUDIED HIM?

TRUST ME. I KNOW THE TYPE.

WHY DID YOU...?

BECAUSE, LATER...

...YOU MIGHT NOT BE ABLE TO DO THAT.

THOOM
THOOM

THAT'S MY CUE.

GOOD LUCK.

I have to keep him contained, so he can't *fly*.

I yell at him to keep him distracted.

LISTEN TO ME.

The *Green K* in the ring slows his reflexes.

I'VE OPENED A GAS MAIN. IF YOU SO MUCH AS MAKE A SPARK WITH YOUR HEAT VISION--

--YOU'LL BLOW UP THE ENTIRE BLOCK.

WAM

If I hit him again, I'll shatter every bone in *my* hand. The *Kevlar* only protects so much.

AND YOU *KNOW* WHAT BUILDING WE'RE UNDER.

BTAM

YOU HURT ME.

THIS ENDS NOW.

LOOK UP.

YOU CAN SAVE *HER.* OR FIGHT ME. IT IS *YOUR* CHOICE. *NOT* POISON IVY'S.

Come on, Clark.

Be the Boy Scout.

The *Metropolis Plaza.* Tommy and I stayed here as kids.

PUT THE MONEY *DOWN.*

YOU'RE GOING BACK TO GOTHAM CITY.

LIKE *HELL* I--

--*AM.*

I'VE ALREADY CALLED MY OLD FRIEND *MAGGIE SAWYER.*

SHE'S ARRANGED FOR THE *METROPOLIS S.C.U.* TO DELIVER YOU TO THE *G.C.P.D.*

I DON'T KNOW *HOW* YOU FOUND ME, BUT --

Jim Lee's pencils were used on the cover to the second printing.

JEPH LOEB is the author of BATMAN: THE LONG HALLOWEEN, BATMAN: DARK VICTORY, SUPERMAN FOR ALL SEASONS, *Spider-Man: Blue* and *Daredevil: Yellow*. A writer/producer living in Los Angeles, his credits include *Teen Wolf, Commando, Buffy: The Animated Series* and *Smallville*.

JIM LEE was born in Seoul, South Korea in 1964. He graduated from Princeton University with a degree in psychology but decided to try his hand at comic-book art — his childhood fantasy. He found work at Marvel Comics, where his work quickly proved so popular that the company created a new X-Men title just to show-case it. In 1992, Lee formed his own comics company, WildStorm Productions, which became one of the founding components of Image Comics. There, he launched the best-selling WILDC.A.T.S and introduced scores of new characters such as GEN13. He also helped to discover and train a phalanx of writers, artists, and colorists. With its steady success, WildStorm as a business grew so demanding that Lee found he no longer had any time to draw, leading to his decision to sell the company to DC Comics. He remains WildStorm's editorial director but now concentrates on his first love, art. He lives in La Jolla, California with his wife Angie and his daughters Tyler, Kelsey and Siena.

BIOGRAPHIES

SCOTT WILLIAMS has worked with Jim Lee for more than ten years, and he was voted Favorite Inker for five years in a row (1990-94) in the *Comics Buyer's Guide* Fan Awards. His inking work can be found in WILDCATS, GEN13, JUST IMAGINE STAN LEE... WONDER WOMAN, WILDCATS/X-MEN, *X-Men: Mutant Genesis,* and *X-Men: X-Tinction Agenda.*

ALEX SINCLAIR bought his first comic book — DETECTIVE COMICS #500 — with his brother, Celes, at the local con-venience store. He immediately fell in love with comics and with Batman, who continues to be his favorite character. (Alex and Celes still argue over who would win in a fight between Batman and Superman.) He has previously worked on KURT BUSIEK'S ASTRO CITY, TOP 10, HARLEY QUINN, and, with Jim Lee and Scott Williams, on WILDC.A.T.S, GEN13, and DIVINE RIGHT. Sinclair lives in San Diego with his sidekick Rebecca and their four hench-girls: Grace, Blythe, Meredith, and Harley. He would love to fight crime, but the weather's too nice...

RICHARD STARKINGS is best known as the creator of the Comicraft studio, purveyors of unique design and fine lettering — and a copious catalogue of comic-book fonts — since 1992. He is less well known as the creator and publisher of *Hip Flask* and his semi-autobiographical cartoon strip, *Hedge Backwards*. He never seems to get tired of reminding people that he lettered BATMAN: THE KILLING JOKE with a pen.